Becoming Media Critics

By Samita Nandy

The views and opinions expressed herein are those of the author and do not necessarily reflect the positions of the publisher.

© 2019 Samita Nandy, Ph.D.

All rights reserved

Front and back cover photographs and design:

© 2019 WaterHill Publishing, Toronto

All rights reserved

ISBN: 978-1-7753096-2-8

Table of Contents

HOW TO DEVELOP MEDIA AND PUBLIC RELATIONS.............4

WHAT IS A PERSONA BRAND? 5

MEDIA EXAMPLES 8

CRITIC OR COMMENTATOR 9

MEDIA AND PUBLIC RELATIONS: HOW TO BE A CRITIC 11

PUBLIC RELATIONS (PR) 12

SOCIAL MEDIA 14

EDITORIAL BEATS 15

HOW TO COMMUNICATE WITH A JOURNALIST 15

TELLING YOUR STORY 16

INTERVIEW EXCERPTS...20

STYLE OF STORIES: STORY WRITING OR STORY TELLING 29

OP-ED PITCH LETTER SAMPLE 32

OP-ED PUBLICATION SAMPLE #1 36

OP-ED SAMPLE PUBLICATION #2 42

REFERENCES 44

Becoming Media Critics

Introduction:

How to Develop Media and Public Relations

During the Centre for Media and Celebrity Studies' (CMCS) annual conferences, speakers highlighted how models, actors, authors, and athletes are using aesthetics to communicate stories and build their brand persona – including stylizing their profile pictures. Similarly, expressing personal style and taste through clothing has played a key role in publicizing and promoting brands. To be clear, their brand success lies not in the combination of visual and literary expressions of fashion but rather the overall *style* they adopt to raise their *voice* in media and public relations.

The question becomes: How can we – as writers, artists or activists – develop media and public relations to give voice to our artistic or social causes?

This guidebook draws on my experience and practical insights that I have used for successful media outreach and that was shared in my media workshop "Scholars as Critics." It is aimed at those who are advocating for an urgent cause, where personal values act as grounding principles and go hand-in-hand with competence.

The learning outcomes of this guide include:

- An introduction to media and public relations
- Determining whether you need a publicist
- Understanding why visual and performing artists and writers should become media critics
- Appreciating the importance of using social and traditional media to build your brand

Let's start by taking a look at branding and then media and public relations, where branding figures heavily.

What is a Persona Brand?

A persona brand is a collection of personality traits, values, beliefs, and attitudes – an identity – that your brand consistently reveals to help connect with a target audience. While it may not lead to commercial exchange, it can act as cultural capital (Nandy, 2015).[1] For example, expressions, or content created by the persona (such as art pieces tied to profile pictures, titles, and professional summaries or activism) can hold brand value (Wheaton & Nandy, 2015).[2] Why? Because branded personas reflect and reinforce individual experiences and resonate with audiences.

Note:

- Professional titles (e.g., author, actor) are markers of a brand persona, whereby the brand is distinguishing and indicates value. Academic and professional workplaces offer a variety of possibilities to build a persona through acquiring expertise.

In more detail, a brand can foster bonding when the persona is viewed as authentic.[3] For example, the CMCS board member, Dr Anita Krajnc bonded with Hollywood actor, Joaquin Phoenix over an animal vigil in Los Angeles. Later, Canadian national media covered his support for her (growing) *Save Movement* in Toronto.[4] Krajnc's brand persona as an activist did not gain visibility due to a celebrity-led campaign. Rather, her authenticity in giving water to dehydrated pigs and winning a related court case built her brand persona and her *Save Movement* that celebrity activists view as authentic and meaningful.

Photography: Jo-Anne McArthur

Alternatively, in celebrity culture, the gap is widening between the *self* and the *persona*. On the one hand, it seems morally permissible to use a certain aesthetic language to develop a personality brand. After all, language is a symbolic mode of communication that does not always lend itself to precision or to a clear understanding.

But when we – as writers– build a brand persona through media and public relations, we have to ask ourselves: What is our authentic message or cause? Through what medium, form, and style can we most effectively give voice to that message?

To build a brand that carries and helps to disseminate that message, we need to:

- Nurture effective media and public relations
- Build research profiles
- Showcase our personalities through content and brand surrogates

In building a brand persona, media relations and online identities act as cultural capital to establish successful careers in education, art, and advocacy. When you build a brand through social and traditional media and public relations, it may not offer direct financial compensation but it does offer symbolic value and cultural capital over time.

On a personal note, before I applied for graduate school, I had conversations with faculty members who consistently expressed enthusiasm about my media contributions. That is why I chose to always include my online portfolios, media experience, and relationships as part of my applications, even in the post-doctoral phase of my work.

Media Examples

These are some examples of my media appearances at the Toronto International Film Festival (in Canada), where I was interviewed by journalists from the Canadian broadcasting companies CP24 and CTV. While I was engaged in activism at the ReelWorld Film Festival (also in Toronto), I was quoted by The Telegraph and interviewed by CBC and SUN TV. Eventually, Chatelaine and Flare magazines and other media outlets contacted me for interviews.

In most cases, I did not submit a press release to get on the radar of media representatives and I have never had a publicist. Instead, I simply attended events that I was passionate about and I expressed a willingness to speak up about the main issues when I was asked to comment. Later, I expressed informed opinions on social media where journalists are also present. Even if you choose to have a publicist, you still need to know the basics of media and public relations. You need to know how media relations work, what to expect in terms of interview questions, and why are you are raising your voice as a critic.

At this point, you may be wondering: How is this different from being a commentator?

Critic or Commentator?

Being a commentator is more objective than being a critic, as a commentator does not always have an individual voice. For example, the use of "I agree" in the following press clip is an example of a statement that has an opinion but does not have the power to mobilize social or personal change:

> "He gave a news conference and he called his phone call with Ukraine's president 'perfect.' Then Nancy Pelosi said, 'I agree. It was fantastic.'" — *CONANonan O'BRIENrien*[5]

In contrast, the following arguments (as well as the interview and op-ed at the end of the guide) offer criticism with the help of opinionated words. These action-driven words activate brand building and media / public relations for change:

> "I told myself, Malala, you have already faced death. This is your second life. Don't be afraid — if you are afraid, you can't move forward."
>
> "The Taliban could take our pens and books, but they couldn't stop our minds from thinking."
>
> — Malala Yousafzai[6]
>
> "For 25 years, countless people have come to the U.N. climate conferences begging our world leaders to stop emissions, and clearly that has not worked as emissions are continuing to rise. So I will not beg the world leaders to care for our future. [...] When haters go after your looks and differences, it means they have nowhere left to go. And then you know you're winning!"
>
> – Greta Thunberg[7]
>
> "I will instead let them know change is coming whether they like it or not."
>
> – Greta Thunberg[8]

Given these considerations, it is important to address some common misconceptions:

- Criticism is not about being negative or absolute

- Being a critic involves putting ideas into context (like a reviewer), using arguments and counter-arguments
- While a critique can be neutral, it is not the same thing as a commentary (which is more of a report or statement of facts)

I strongly recommend being a critic and expressing your opinions through the media. By being trained as critics, writers, artists, and activists can not only add more perspective but also a persuasive edge to discussions. In the process, the critic can disseminate research and change practices in a way that validates their career.

Media and Public Relations: How to Be a Critic?

- Identify your area of expertise
- Create a media database
- Craft your pitch
- Build relationships with media organizations
- Write about topics that you are an expert in
- Engage in public speaking and create reels
- Create a community (or a following) around your ideas
- Develop a media portfolio (e.g., website, press kit, and media clips)

Let's say that your objective is to develop a record of your media and public relations experiences. For this, it is important to be clear on the following key terms:

Public Relations (PR)

- Protects public personalities, studios, networks, and production companies by turning ideas into published/broadcasted social data that can be accepted, negotiated, or resisted in the public sphere
- Has two components – promotion and publicity
- Examples include press releases, bio, high-resolution photos, and media pitches

One question I am often asked is "Do public relations start with media?" Quite simply, it can start with a megaphone on the street, a microphone on stage, from behind a camera documenting stories, or giving a voice to an activist in a group. In my case, it started with a documentary film and an associated press release. Given that my topic was of public interest, I received grants and media coverage for my work. Based on what I learned, my university-affiliated board members and I launched the Centre for Media and Celebrity Studies (CMCS). As a non-profit media organization under the provincial Government of Ontario, it facilitates research and media commentaries for both the public and academic communities. I also wrote a monograph, book chapters, and op-eds tailored to the general public.

I don't wait for the media to help me build my relationships with the public. I engage and mobilize the public through talks and social media outreach, fostering engagement that is supportive and open to the media covering us. My personal philosophy is that <u>public relations are human relations</u>. It starts with human stories and reaching out to journalists in a way that is authentic and caring.

In a word, you can be your own PR rep. This will enable you to hire a PR professional for larger projects, and they can work with you as an equal to harness the potential of your audience and collaborate with you.

The key message here is to **reach out with a story and give it a personal voice**.

As a case in point, I shared an opinion piece related to the #MeToo movement with *Feminism in India* and *Brown Girl Magazine*. At the end of this guide, I will share how I reached out and connected with my pitch letter so that you have a model to follow.

At this point, I bet you're thinking "why didn't you pitch to the *New York Times* or the *Guardian*?" Although I have high regard for these outlets (and recommend reaching out to the columnists and editors of the news section your topic relates to), I was too impatient to wait and follow up with them. This actually turned out to be a blessing in disguise. I learned that media outreach is not about being perfect – it is about what's right for you and your cause at any given time. It is about connecting with your audience, or in this case readership, and building a relationship with them on a topic that matters to you both.

With this background information in place, I now want to draw your attention to social media and editorial best practices.

Social Media

Building your social media profile involves the consistent use of:

- Twitter, LinkedIn, Facebook, and Instagram (selected based on where your target audience is located)
- Blogs
- Podcasts
- Online videos and photographs (shared through platforms like Instagram and Facebook)

Note: Your social media username and / or content must reflect your area of expertise. For example, my Twitter handle is "famecritic" as I am a critic of fame.

In terms of generating content and connecting with your audience, your editorial mission is to determine:

- Who is your core audience?
- What will you deliver to them?
- How can you best package it?

- What is your desired outcome?

Editorial Beats

- Research
- Get community perspectives
- Practice

How to Communicate with a Journalist?

- Start by expressing gratitude to the interviewer for inviting your views
- Enjoy the opportunity to share your message and express it through verbal & non-verbal cues
- Be confident, positive, and concise
- Never say "no comment"
- If a question or comment is out of scope, be honest about it
- Stick to your key message and expertise – do not offer educated guesses
- Have 3 keywords/sub-messages you can refer to
- Is there a personal or social change connected to your cause that you could tie it to?
- Is your message inspiring and uplifting?
- Avoid jargon

Telling your Story

How can your story nurture social change? What is involved in the art of storytelling, both in literal and visual forms?

I had the privilege of reflecting on several poignant articles on this topic that a researcher in celebrity studies, Kirsty Fairclough kindly shared on Twitter. Her posts opened my eyes and helped me get reacquainted with the vision that my mum and dad had for me while they lived in Canada and in India: equality.

Fairclough also shared feminist author Chimamanda Ngozi Adichie's TED talk "The Danger of a Single Story."[9] In this talk, Adichie describes how a dominant narrative dispose of and systematically 'others' voices and does so from a position of entitlement and privilege. While this is often done in ways that are not consciously recognized, this kind of narrative seeks difference instead of commonality.

As writers or readers, if our goals are related to learning, informing, or connecting, we must ensure that we are speaking to something common, rather than alienating or 'othering' – while using our own artistic style.

I trust that each of us can find much more that we have in common with each other to discuss than what divides us. And sometimes, in order to truly connect, our own 'style' of giving a voice to a story needs to change.

Of course, style is about more than fashion or trends. Even red-carpet events see celebrities expressing political statements in stylized forms, above and beyond glamorous fashion.[10]

At the same time, actors and models are now developing a *style* of offering opinions beyond the fashion that was traditionally associated with their fame. So much so, in fact, that many of them have become influencers without having expertise on the matters they discuss.[11]

Is this *style* of voice better than well-crafted and thoughtfully researched evidence from positions that Chimamanda Ngozi Adichie would critique?

My short answer is "yes and no."

Written words have the power to categorize and discriminate – to 'other' and wipe out multiple stories in favor of influence and privilege. No wonder online bullying occurs so frequently, given the accessibility, reach, and relative anonymity of social media. In a recent Skype chat that I conducted, journalist Janet Johnson said, quite appropriately, that the public, including academics and other writers and artists, were never taught to have a voice. If we do not have a voice, how can we give one to others? As Johnson further pointed out, many entitled social media users were not prepared to handle or cope with new voices who competed with their opinions and world-views when social media exploded in 2007.

That being said, our own stylistic art of storytelling in non-verbal, aesthetic forms of communication also has the power to create more equality and support democratic practices – by opening up discussions in a variety of spaces that help move society towards more progressive thoughts.

In my experience of viewing feminist photography and visual narratives, I question the monolithic style used to represent female models in our image-obsessed celebrity culture. Irrespective of whether they are clothed or not, females are often photographed in static forms that are not far removed from the nude Pre-Raphaelites that were used to satisfy the male sexual appetite and gaze in the Early Renaissance period.

Emma Hope Allwood invites us to reconsider this in her recent article.[12]

You can also read more on this topic in Fairclough's post.[13]

In my experience, the male gaze is unconsciously present and widening social gaps, even when I do not have a man photographing me.

Here are some ideas to consider in thinking about how to bridge these gaps:

1) Tell your story in a style that has the capacity to point out Adichie's 'commonalities' rather than 'differences in humanity.' Your art of storytelling might be related to rare contexts, times, roles, relationships, and/or non-verbal communication that might have touched you during your travels, literally or metaphorically. For this practice, I recommend setting aside at least 30 minutes a day to write and to start with a blog. Note, most of my blogs begin as Instagram posts

and then become converted into videos that see more engagement.

2) Describe a social cause (not a single-issue) that is part of your story.

One of the challenges in this Information Age is that there are so many worthy causes that, due to time restrictions or branding needs, we must choose those that are closest to our authentic selves. The best way to navigate this is by identifying the overlapping roots of the many causes we are interested in.

To see what I mean, it is helpful to review these interview excerpts from the Hollywood and Bollywood actor and Oscar-voter, Kabir Bedi.

Source: http://samitanandy.com/kabirbedi-interview

Interview Excerpts

Kabir Bedi: "One believes in certain causes. I believe in the cause of education. I believe in the cause of helping and preventing blindness. India has one of the largest blind populations in the world. And if something can be prevented, that is the best thing you can do. I am involved in the educational aspects [of helping to prevent the prevalence and incidence of blindness in India].

I use all the social media that I have [access to] to talk about myself as well as promote the causes that interest me.

[Is] what I say disseminated widely enough? Probably not. But, by the same token, it is proportionate to the amount of time I put into disseminating that news.

Instead of just putting them [the causes] on Facebook, Instagram, and Twitter, I can go to all kinds of different forums. [I don't do this] because, frankly, [I don't have the time] to make the causes my full-time job. And therefore, I just put out there what I believe in... the things I hope for. And I hope that those who are following me will take the message [and carry it forward].

There are a lot of causes in this world – one can't do all of them – one chooses the ones [to focus on where] they can make a difference. The ones that I am involved in – I have certainly seen a great difference... it has improved fundraising, it has improved the morale of the people in the field… the results [have been] spectacular. This is real, tangible change.

When you know that so many thousands of people are saved from blindness because of surgical interventions that happened – that prevented them from going blind – you know you have done good. The rest is numbers – it doesn't matter if you help 1 person, 1000, or 10000; the main thing is the processes. So one has to work with the reach one has. But hope that the reach amplifies itself through those people that are part of [it]."

Samita Nandy: "And I think what makes it very real and engaging is a lot of the life stories that come along – the contexts in which you write – what you observe in parallel to the causes that you are fighting for. I think that makes it very authentic. Being a living example of change is the most important thing, [to paraphrase] Gandhi. Bearing witness is something he always advocated for. I believe that regardless – every voice counts, every step counts – so to put it out there [your voice] along with your authentic stories, your contexts, is very powerful. Because one of the biggest issues that I noticed in tabloid journalism is the loss of the contexts in which a lot of work, whether it is artistic, activist, or just educational emerges. The nuances and subtleties are lost. But I think that's [also] what makes the voices very original.

Another issue that I noticed in general – in education, art, and activism – is that we use a lot of words but it becomes more powerful when you have certain images and [...] facts along with them. ... The reason why images are powerful is that they act as an aesthetic mode of communication. They are not rational; they are not linear. While rationality has really allowed progressive thinking... the same rationality and linear thinking have also made categorization and discrimination possible. According to a TED talk that I watched, artistic modes of inquiries are very important – anything that is sensed, perceived can bring emotional, human responses that rational words can standardize or categorize in favor of a dominant ideology.

What came out of the last conference that I hosted is how fashion can act as an activist tool in pop culture. We are focusing on popular culture and how tabloid journalism is dealing with it. Fashion, particularly glamorous fashion, is coming into question. Most people have social media profiles, they stylize and re-fashion themselves and re-contextualize themselves. So, in my mind, fashion can act as a political tool to bring change. This is very non-verbal, it is aesthetic (e.g., what Bibi Russell has done).

Kabir Bedi: "It is an area of great interest [to me]. My wife and I are part of the sustainable fashion movement. They had a number of events in India to promote the fair trade concept, to promote sustainable fashion – [like asking] who makes your clothes? Asking those questions makes manufacturers more aware of the possibilities of the [community] efforts. In fact, as a result of those efforts, Mumbai Fashion Week has one section entirely on sustainable fashion. So the message of sustainable fashion is spreading, as it should spread.

Because not only are we talking about the ethics of using underpaid labor but also of using products that are more natural. So that is an important movement – more of my wife's area of interest – Parveen Dusanj Bedi's. But I support the concept fully. I go to their events, show my presence, and I hope that the message spreads."

Samita Nandy: "I feel that the stories around fashion – or even using fabric within fashion as a text to read in fashion – has a strong potential to reach out [to the community] compared to… rumors, scandals, and gossip. I think there is an alternative space that fashion can [open up and facilitate]. I have hope there too."

Kabir Bedi: "The real scandal is not who slept with whom. The real scandal is [that] when that building collapsed in Bangladesh [it showed] the extent of exploitation in the fashion world: how many big names are involved and how many of those names have become responsive today as a result of that accident and loss of life. So there is a movement and I am sure it will pick up a lot of steam.

Even in Bombay, plastic is banned and people have started using paper bags.

It's just a matter of will, a desire to see a slightly different world. And that's what's happening at all levels – at private levels, at government levels. The only thing is that we have to get some aspects of the industry that still hold on to the old order – that still want to be exploitative, that still want to pollute, that still want to be purely driven by profit. And those people will eventually lose their popularity because people's consciousness is moving in a different direction."

Samita Nandy: "Along with the question of fashion activism, do you feel that there are limitations [that come] with its potential? What are the limits of fashion activism?"

Kabir Bedi: "The limits of fashion activism are:

1. There are manufacturers who are not interested in the topic and just want to profit

2. There are customers [who] are, frankly, not interested in the larger goals – they just want the cheapest clothes they can get.

So, as long this alliance between the manufacturer wanting more profits and the consumer wanting the lowest cost continues, then that becomes a limitation. However, if it's clear that there is a social trend against that and that social movement makes such manufacturers uncomfortable and unattractive to the customers, these things will change. There are certainly obstacles [, however].

Samita Nandy: "Do you feel that universities could help when it comes to fashion activism or just fashion journalism? What kind of role can universities play?"

Kabir Bedi: "I think universities need to, in addition to imparting the very valuable knowledge that they do, make students in all subjects [aware] of the social dimensions of what they propose to do – whether that is journalism, whether that is fashion, whether that is sports, whether that is cinema…. And there is a social responsibility for promoting a shared good, which is part of the human condition. We must help each other a lot. And if those things are made clear by the educators, they will lead to students who are more enlightened, therefore becoming better citizens of the world."

Samita Nandy: "Do you think more hands-on work, more fieldwork, would really help as opposed to just teaching theory?"

Kabir Bedi: "Fieldwork obviously helps but fieldwork is expensive and it takes a lot of time. The experience is important but even before the experience, the information is more important. Those [who] have the sensibility [to consider]: 'Oh my god, there is this damage to this. My god, I didn't think about that and will use that information to improve things in the world, in society, in the products I use.' They will make the biggest difference. But you can't just bank on fieldwork. You have to allow for the information itself to be the biggest influencer.

Gone are the days when parents were the only source of information 'Daddy, why is the sky blue?' and daddy says 'the sky is blue because of XYZ.' Now [children] Google it. Google is the biggest parent today, as far as information goes. Parents have other very valuable functions. But one thing is people are not imprisoned by beliefs, dogmas, and circumstances anymore if they do not want to [be]. They have too much reach around them for information, for new directions. And that's why mentoring people to understand what is available is the single most important thing [you can do as an educator].

It's like that old saying, 'give a man a fish, you feed him for a day. [If you] teach a man how to fish, [you] teach him how to feed [himself] for a lifetime.' Teach people what's out there so that they know what's out there because the biggest sin of all is ignorance in today's Information Age. And that's the job of an educator – to [help students] overcome that ignorance whatever form that takes."

Samita Nandy: "In giving that information, do you feel that images – telling visual stories – would be effective instead of just reading books?"

Kabir Bedi: "Of course. Stories are always the most effective form [to use to share information] as people have seen stories. Cinema has done its share. Today people are aware of 'blood diamonds' because there are films that are made on the subject…. The fact that people are aware of the Bangladesh tragedy is because people saw pictures of the buildings collapsing and people being pulled out from there. So if things are put in an audiovisual way, it magnifies the impact – there is no question. We are living in an audio-visual world – never forget that part of the world."

Samita Nandy: "Media educators could use storytelling for social change, especially when media and educational institutions are limited to specific research agendas and news agendas. The reason why I think that way is because a lot of the discrimination I observe is based on looks. When it comes to discrimination or there is bias against race, gender, species, or age it's really around looks. And I feel visual storytelling and images in that storytelling would really help [to combat this discrimination]. What is your take on that?"

Kabir Bedi: "Well, you are absolutely right. That's also the part of the job of educators – that you just don't give people information. You have to enable people to spread that information. You have to make them facilitators. And the best way to make them facilitators is the use of storytelling. People love listening to stories. You can't just give a set of facts that they are not interested in. But you can link them together in a story that is fascinating. [They] will absorb [the information] without realizing it. So one of the great jobs of educators today is to make [the] 'doers' of tomorrow into storytellers."

Samita Nandy: "We come from an oral history…."

Kabir Bedi: "Oral history is, of course, important but now we have the written word, we have audio, we have visual – we have all aspects [required for storytelling]. Earlier, people used to come to meetings with a few things written on a piece of paper in their agenda. Today, they come with PowerPoint presentations… mini-movies and brilliant slideshows. [These practices are not reserved for] the common human – even in boardrooms, storytelling is a very important device. People love listening to stories. It's one of the oldest things – sitting under a tree and listening to a wise, old [person] telling stories. And that ability to tell stories is an art.

What is storytelling? What is a story? A good story, in its essence, has conflict – something that must happen when something [else] cannot. The stronger the 'must,' the stronger the 'cannot,' the stronger 'the story.' This is the way [educators must] put things. So teaching the art of storytelling of how to take information and turn it into a story that people want to see or listen to is an art and that is one of the big jobs of communicators today, and of educators today, and of parents. Teachers and mentors: we need a world that is full of storytellers."

Style of Stories: Story Writing or Story Telling?

As a writer, I believe in writing about causes in my stories and publishing them for a broad audience. But sometimes, I am limited on time and cannot always rely on words, because they can fail us (for reasons outlined earlier). Moreover, when empowering or inspiring others, we have to keep in mind that they might engage better with words that are not written down. In any case, as Dr Kabir Bedi emphasized, we need more storytellers, and images must be prioritized in public relations messaging, which are often driven by stories and facts.

So let's focus on storytelling and the stylistic art of being conversational (or simply expressive) even in our media pitches and published media articles. Remember the old saying that a picture tells 1,000 words? There is a lot of wisdom contained in this statement.

Now, I want to talk to you about how to develop your authentic style in giving a voice in media and public relations. This is not always a matter of using fashion but rather re-fashioning a dominant form of storytelling, i.e., exclusively relying on words or just using photographs. More broadly, it is our dominant social narrative in educational and workplaces that trains our perception to only see a writer, actor, or any other creative professional in one light. But if you carefully go through the biographies of well-known artists (e.g., Madonna, Beyoncé, Woody Allen, and Andy Warhol), they used their various artistic backgrounds and recycled their styles as expressions to cross-promote their story in a unique style, beyond labels. Tabloids may even label them as eccentric, but that also helps to attract audiences who are interested in extraordinary experiences.

All of that is to say you know and own your truth. You have a unique style of combining media content and methods that is specific to your authentic call, even if it breaks the rules of other people's formulas. In fact, breaking the rules is one of the only ways to stand out and reach your audience with your message. You can use various methods to help you find the call of your style – including travel, serendipitous encounters, and nonverbal expressions that feel pleasurable and passionate.

Don't just tell your audience your views – allow them to 'feel' them and connect with you on a personal level. Your audience will be more interested in feeling and connecting with 'you' rather than repeating what they know already.

For example, journalist Stewart Rogers uses his passionate music to disseminate his messages. My serendipitous discovery of this practice, while I was at a workshop in Lisbon, motivated me to start using my 1-min fashion films in presentations. They are a combination of still and moving images, paired with Spanish and Latino music I discovered on my personal journeys that called to me. I used them to portray feminist modeling, using media to tell stories and to give a voice to this issue through music and my visual evidence.[14]

We are now at the end of this short guide that covered images beyond written words. Ironically, I am running out of words to use in my storytelling. Before I go on to share my pitch letter and published op-ed as an example of successful media outreach, I encourage you to check out my videos at www.imdb.com/me/samitanandy. A Google search of my name, Samita Nandy, will generate more results in its video and image feed.

I hope my published story below gives a sample format that you can use to tell your story and advocate for your cause in media and public relations.

Op-Ed Pitch Letter Sample

Dear Feminism in India (FII) team,

I came across the critical feminist voice that FII magazine offers and wanted to reach out with my story.

In my post-doctoral research, the rise of social media celebrities, online sexual harassment and teen suicide has prompted a compelling question: is our understanding of fame lacking? Or, conversely, do we understand it too well?

One thing is clear: the vast majority of women have struggled to find a voice.

And despite my PhD in fame, I've faced the same sexual harassment that many celebrities have experienced in Bollywood and Hollywood's post-Weinstein era.

Yes, #MeToo.

My education, career and personal experiences have taught me a great deal about speaking up as an Indian woman today. I overcame the harassment I faced both personally and professionally, and launched the Centre for Media and Celebrity Studies (CMCS) in order to make celebrity studies readily available to the public. Today the CMCS serves thousands of members, empowering women to enjoy the creative and financial control they previously lacked.

Unfortunately, I've also found that harassment can start in the family for the sake of honour – a historical notion in celebrity culture as well. This raises a serious social problem, and the lack of humanity in 'pseudo killings' calls for the urgent understanding of what many people want: fame, even it if it is for the sake of family nobility.

This brings me to my pitch. Would you be interested in a 1,500-word personal essay that connects sexual harassment and the dismissal of women to celebrity culture? The essay will ultimately detail the challenges of finding a voice as a woman. What makes my case different, however, is that despite the lack of evidence observed at times in the #MeToo Movement, I reveal real names, use first-hand witnesses as ethnographic data and explore social causes.

In short, I hope my experiences and achievements in the US, Canada, Australia and India will inspire women who feel silenced and excluded. I intend to interview international film star Kabir Bedi and celebrity studies scholar Dr David Marshall for the story – he has appeared on ABC Radio National – in addition to other experts. This essay will not only break myths, but also provide actual tools to help women rise in popular culture.

About Me: As the Director of Centre for Media and Celebrity Studies (CMCS), keynote speaker and author of Fame in Hollywood North, I have written for The Globe and Mail, Excalibur News and Celebrity Studies journal. My doctoral research at Curtin University in Australia has led to several interviews in media outlets including CBC, CTV Breaking News, CP24, CITY TV News, SUN Media, 24 Hours, VICE, Flare, Chatelaine,

Hollywood North Magazine, Yahoo! Entertainment, and many others. I am currently writing a novel – the first book in a trilogy addressing the ways women can become celebrity activists in the post-Weinstein era of Hollywood. You can find more information on my website: www.samitanandy.com.

Thank you for your time and consideration. I would be honoured to work with you on this piece, and will gladly answer any questions you may have. In addition, I'll be happy to submit a draft of the full essay on request.

Sincerely,

Dr Samita Nandy

Director, Centre for Media and Celebrity Studies
Keynote & Author, Fame in Hollywood North (WaterHill)
PhD Curtin University, Australia (Celebrity)
MA & BA York University. Canada (Communication & Media)
www.cmc-centre.com @celeb_studies
www.samitanandy.com @famecritic

Media (Selected): The Globe and Mail, CBC, CTV Breaking News CP 24, SUN Media, 24 Hours News, CITY TV News, VICE, Chatelaine, Flare, Hollywood North Magazine, FUSIA, ANOKHI, Starbuzz, Humber News, Hamilton Arts and Letters, Canadian Journalism Foundation, ATN Television, CINA 1650 AM, VoiceAmerica Women, Share magazine, Eternity Watch magazine, Brampton Guardian, and 'Daytime' on Rogers Television. ANDA (Brazil), Nippon TV (Japan). Also, published in *Celebrity Studies* journal editions and in *Persona Studies*.

CELEBRITY 101

For the academics who study Kim, Madonna and Kanye, celebs are serious business

BRAD HUNTER
POSTMEDIA NETWORK

Kim. Kanye. Jennifer. Brad. Madonna.

Celebrity culture has become so ubiquitous that we're on a first-name basis.

And for a growing coterie of academics, the study of that culture and its wider implications is a full-time pursuit.

Dr. Samita Nandy's life work has been putting stars under glass and drawing lines between the celeb bubble and the wider culture.

"Celebrities give us an opportunity to self-reflect," the Toronto-based academic told 24 Hours. "And celebrity studies tend to draw on their shared and points of view."

Nandy is the director of the Centre for Media and aid

Celebrity Studies, a virtual think-tank that has more than 1,000 members and holds conferences around the world.

And what CMCS does is "shed light on the celebrity process behind the scant biographical details." It even publishes a Celebrity Studies journal.

Nandy was first drawn to the world of celebrities as a child watching the bold and colourful movies of Bollywood. Her inspiration? Nandy's own mother was an actress in the Indian movie machine.

And lest you think the bad for all thing celebrity is reserved for English-speaking countries, you'd be wrong. On magazine racks from Barcelona to Beijing colourful tabloids scream out pushing, flattering and chasing the local superstars.

But the game has changed.

"While celebrity culture has ebbed and flowed over the decades

Dr. Samita Nandy, SUPPLIED

been bigger.

"We now know the persona behind Kim Kardashian. We know a lot about what she likes, what she wears and what she doesn't like," Nandy said.

"Social media is letting us experience that culture in a different way, it's more personal."

tion of Andy Warhol's maxim that: "In the future, everyone will be world famous for 15 minutes." It is the province of the *Bachelor* contestant who's booted after a couple episodes, or as *The Simpsons* satirized, the "I didn't do it, kid."

Except, according to Nandy, "15 minutes is now 15 seconds."

Moreover, celebrity is reserved for the enterprising comics, jugglers and ringers who live and die by YouTube. Nandy says there aren't in the Jennifer Aniston stratosphere but are famous nonetheless, but less so.

"These people's fame doesn't transfer to traditional media. And you don't even have to be talented," Nandy said, adding that their fame is driven by social media and nothing else.

"Social media offers a democratic platform to share what's not found elsewhere," Nandy said, adding that stars use social media to buff their reps. "It can help you be known for good deeds (see Angelina Jolie) rather than notoriety."

Nandy was quick to point out that social media plays a key role in connecting celebrities to wider issues. Whether it's Leo and the environment, Angelina and refugees or Lady Gaga supporting LGBTQ rights, our power can makes a difference.

Just a single tweet from Justin Bieber can trigger support for a worthy cause.

"Celebrity activities can

notice and and help regular people understand complex issues," she said "And it can help fans understand the person behind the celebrity."

Now, Nandy is turning her eyes northward for a new book entitled *Fame in Hollywood North* where she tackles celebrity culture in Canada. The book is out in August.

"Fame is very different in Canada," Nandy said, adding that Quebec is an outlier because of its national identity. "But we have had a profound influence on American culture."

Canadians are at once forced to be similar to Americans — and different.

"Canadians are much more conservative than Americans but a little too prissy," she said. "Hopefully, some day soon we can drop the prissiness."

Op-Ed Publication Sample #1

How I Overcame My Trauma and Found My Voice[15]

Trigger warning: Sexual abuse, Violence

By Samita Nandy

I left abusive environments to pursue an education and embark on my path to earning a PhD in fame. My goal? To honour my mother, who was forbidden from becoming a Bollywood film actress and stage dancer on the grounds of sexism, and to overcome the harassment I continually faced in my own life. After receiving my PhD, I went on to launch the *Centre for Media and Celebrity Studies* (CMCS), which empowers women to take creative and financial control in the post-Weinstein era of Hollywood. But things weren't always this simple for me. Long before I found my voice, I faced a great deal of inequality as a woman – starting in my own family.

On February 5, 2018 – a year after my father took his last breath – I called my uncle Sailab Nandy. I was nervous about the call. Dark memories washed over me each time I thought about my father's eldest brother Manesh Nandy, who lived with Sailab.

Despite my grandfather's wishes, Manesh – as the firstborn son in British India – believed he was exclusively entitled to the family's multimillion-dollar inheritance. He acquired my uncle Sailab's assets through coercive practices and fraudulent signatures, with the aim of funding his drug-addicted, school-drop-out sons. One of them, Souvik Nandy, demanded that I masturbate him.

I was eight years old at the time.

Yes, #MeToo.

When Manesh answered my call, I found myself at a loss for words. My sense of defeat was fuelled by the lack of evidence surrounding the situation – that, and the challenge of admitting to the sexual harassment permeating our modern family. We had predetermined narratives of love, and sexual harassment didn't reflect those ideals.

"It's Samita. Is Uncle Sailab there?"
"He's out for a few minutes. How are you doing?"
"Well, it's the anniversary of my dad crossing over," I swallowed.
"Yes, yes," he replied, his pitch moving from high to low. Then he chuckled. *"You know, I always thought your dad would have lived way longer than us, but he took his own life."*
"What are you talking about?" I stammered. *"My dad was the most hardworking, positive person I knew!"*
"He was depressed! Why else would he have buried himself in work? Look at the rest of us, enjoying our retired lives."

Before I could share how my father and I loved our café times, cooking at home and travelling together, he overtook my words – just like his son overtook me when he forced my hand on his penis.

"Look, when your father was little, he had typhoid and memory loss. A part of his brain was damaged. You understand, Samita? Damaged!"

"He was a very hardworking person," I retorted, my heart sinking deep in my chest.

"And what about your hard work – your name and fame, as I see on Facebook?"

"I'm working in New York but wish to spend time where my dad wanted to settle – at your home near Calcutta. I feel lonely and want to extend my work in Mumbai. Perhaps I can fly from your home, as Uncle suggested?"

"With the name and fame you have in New York, you should be happy where you are," he said.

Well aware of my international phone bill, I told him I needed to hang up but promised to call back later. And yet the call did not cut off when I said goodbye. In the background I overheard faint voices – the voices of two men who assumed I was no longer there.

"Sailab, listen," chuckled Manesh. *"Samita is a problem. She doesn't know what she wants at this age!"*

Hot tears rolled down my cheeks as he spoke of my dad's only child on the anniversary of his death. I wanted to disconnect the phone, but I needed to hear the truth – no matter how much it hurt to listen.

"Those Western people are obsessed with the material, you know?" said Sailab, breaking my trust then and there.

"Look, she can come in a couple of months," my eldest uncle continued. *"We'll make her sit down and explain that her fantasy won't work. She can visit, but she cannot stay."*

My common-law partner saw me shaking. I still heard my uncles' voices over the phone, but I was no longer listening to their conversation. I had heard everything I needed to hear.

"I am a problem?" I cried, turning to my partner. *"His sons dropped out of school – they were on drugs, they were perverted and abusive – but I am the spoilt kid? My father failed to raise me? Despite my education, despite my trying to please them, this is what they tell me?"*

No matter how educated a woman might be, some will still see to it that she feels powerless. I remember my father telling me this unfortunate truth in Toronto, where I was born.

This was not the first time a woman had been silenced or excluded in my family. My mother's youngest sister was kicked in her pregnant belly by her husband Ananda Dutta in Calcutta. Ironically, he was still put in charge of finalising all the weddings in our family, despite the tensions in his own marriage. In 2015, he verbally abused my aunt – and me and my father, for that matter – when we were asked to share the reasons for our plant-based lifestyle. When we gave him the facts, he yelled and falsified research; he once ran a chicken farm on his terrace, and claimed he knew everything as a result.

I then blurted out my imperfect feminist practice, *"I do not keep men like you in my social circle."*

"See how your father's family is treating me now!" he yelled at his wife. The use of 'father' in this context conjured up images of handing over daughters to strange men, reinforcing patriarchal narratives designed to maintain an imagined sense of male entitlement. Within a few days, my uncle made his wife and son cut all communication with me and my father, in an attempt to silence us. But what can women do when they are muted? How can they succeed despite this kind of abuse?

When I went to Australia in 2006, it was not to pursue a PhD. I'd fallen in love with a man I met online, Iven Taylor, who comforted me after I lost my mother. I became a part of the Taylor family – and Iven was very kind at first. As time went on, however, he began to swear at me, and said that I was "silly," "stupid" or an "idiot" for any and every mundane reason. He even threatened me after I found emails and computer files detailing the various women with whom he'd slept in my absence.

I felt punched hard in the eye after each verbal abuse, but had no evidence of the intimidation. And yet no woman needs to be perfect for justice to be served. The only evidence I had were those 22 computer files that I could not reveal from his property.

"Why do you want to be with me, Samita?" Iven asked in the kitchen after I confronted him. *"You are way up here –"* he raised one arm above his head *"–and I am way down here."*

If any relationship is carried out in fear and under pressure, and there is a lack of individualised choice, it is not rooted in love. I came to realise one does not need to fight for acceptance – we each have the power to speak up and move forward with our lives.

In fear of losing my voice for good, I decided to leave the relationship. Instead of becoming Mrs Taylor, I worked my way towards becoming Dr Nandy. I earned my PhD in fame, founded the CMCS and now take pride in helping other women find a voice in the post-Weinstein era.

'Find a voice' – that's the key phrase here. We stand strong together, but has it been easy? Obviously not. Yet in my life, I managed to change gears and turn adversity into my own version of success. Success is what life can become, no matter how imperfect it is – not what it should be. I trust that's what my parents wished for me when they were alive.

Op-Ed Sample Publication #2

MeToo: Finding my Voice in the Post-Weinstein Era

By Samita Nandy

Content Note: Depicts sexual assault. Names of relatives have been edited for family security.

In Hollywood and Bollywood, fans often pay attention to the #MeToo movement when a story comes from a high-profile movie star. But what happens when one of those fans is a family member hiding abuse inflicted upon you?

You are not alone….

Read full article:
https://www.browngirlmagazine.com/2019/03/metoo-finding-my-voice-post-weinstein-era/

This guide is based on the workshop "Scholars as Critics" as a part of the Centre for Media and Celebrity Studies (CMCS) conference series. CMCS is an international organization and research network that helps coordinating academic research and media commentaries on celebrity culture. CMCS carries a pedagogical philosophy that inspires integration of high-quality research and media skills training in academic and public discourses of fame. The centre believes in intellectual, aesthetic, and ethical values of bridging gaps in higher education and the media industry. Using the critical lens of celebrity studies, CMCS helps coordinating research, publications, productions, and commentaries to mobilize informed opinions in media.

References

1

http://cmc-centre.com/workshops/nyc2015/

2

https://www.taylorfrancis.com/books/e/9781315560519

3

https://torontolife.com/city/life/qa-anita-krajnc-founder-of-toronto-pig-save-on-veganism-animal-rights-and-getting-joaquin-phoenix-to-attend-a-protest/

4

https://globalnews.ca/news/5880660/joaquin-phoenix-joker-vegan-toronto-subway/

5

https://www.nytimes.com/2019/09/26/arts/television/late-night-trump-ukraine-phone-call.html

6

https://www.goodreads.com/work/quotes/24987300

7

https://www.teenvogue.com/story/inspiring-greta-thunberg-quotes-climate-strike-protest

8

https://www.theguardian.com/environment/2018/dec/04/leaders-like-children-school-strike-founder-greta-thunberg-tells-un-climate-summit

9

https://www.ted.com/talks/chimamanda_adichie_the_danger_of_a_single_story?utm_campaign=tedspread&utm_medium=referral&utm_source=tedcomshare

10

https://www.cbc.ca/news/entertainment/political-fashion-red-carpet-1.4964004?cmp=rss

11

http://theconversation.com/how-celebrity-non-experts-and-amateur-opinion-could-change-the-way-we-acquire-knowledge-106002

12

https://www.dazeddigital.com/artsandculture/article/34166/1/why-we-still-need-ways-of-seeing-john-berger

13

https://thelowryblog.wordpress.com/2018/12/21/dr-kirsty-fairclough-on-the-nature-of-celebrity/

14

https://www.imdb.com/name/nm9349098/videoplayer/vi1716829209?ref_=vp_pl_0)

15

https://feminisminindia.com/2019/02/01/overcame-trauma-found-voice/

www.ingramcontent.com/pod-product-compliance
Lightning Source LLC
LaVergne TN
LVHW052256070426
835507LV00035B/3084